Rain and Sun Fun

Written by Katie Nelson

Collins

pink tail

bee

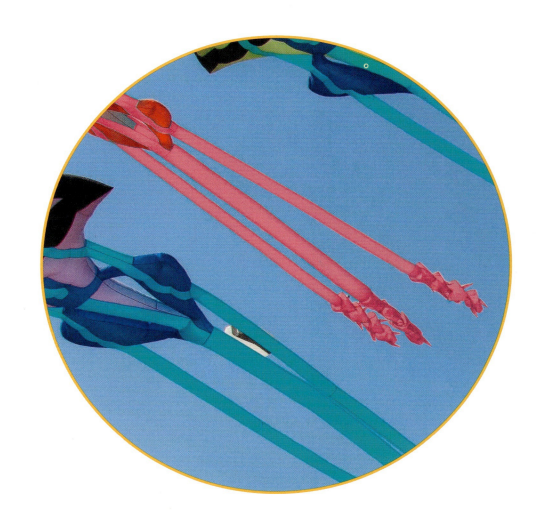

pink tail

bee

a bell
. . . —

a dog in the rain

a bell

a dog in the rain

a red cheek

a light pink hat

a red cheek

a light pink hat

Review: After reading

Use your assessment from hearing the children read to choose any GPCs, words or tricky words that need additional practice.

Read 1: Decoding

- Use grapheme cards to make any words you need to practise. Model reading those words, using teacher-led blending.
- Ask the children to follow as you read the whole book, demonstrating fluency and prosody.

Read 2: Vocabulary

- Look back through the book and discuss the pictures. Encourage the children to talk about details that stand out for them. Use a dialogic talk model to expand on their ideas and recast them in full sentences as naturally as possible.
- Work together to expand vocabulary by naming objects in the pictures that children do not know.
- On page 9, ask the children to find the word that tells us if the weather is dry or wet. (*"rain" tells us it is wet*)

Read 3: Comprehension

- Return to the title page. Ask the children for ideas on alternative titles for the book. (e.g. *Different types of weather; Sun, Rain and Snow*)
- Turn to pages 14 and 15. Encourage the children to describe the pictures. Prompt with questions. For example: What can you play with in the sun? (e.g. *kites*) What sort of animal is in the rain? (*a dog*)